PARENTS' AND TEACHERS' GUIDE

to

by Wendy Heller

CONTENTS

INTRODUCTION

What is the purpose of our lives?

'Abdu'l-Bahá: 'To acquire virtues. We come from the earth; why were we transferred from the mineral to the vegetable kingdom — from the plant to the animal kingdom? So that we may attain perfection in each of these kingdoms, that we may possess the best qualities of the mineral, that we may acquire the power of growing as in the plant, that we may be adorned with the instincts of the animal and possess the faculties of sight, hearing, smell, touch and taste, until from the animal kingdom we step into the world of humanity and are gifted with reason, the power of invention, and the forces of the spirit.' (*Paris Talks*, p. 177)

IF children are to develop their intellectual and spiritual capacities, they need guidance. The *Parents' and Teachers' Guide* to *The Sunshine Tree and Other Tales from Around the World* is designed to help Bahá'í parents and teachers of Bahá'í children's classes in their efforts to provide such guidance for children. Toward this end, the guide offers suggestions for discussion and activities centred around the stories, which illustrate a variety of ideas including qualities to develop — such as kindness to animals, generosity, and perseverance — as well as undesirable patterns to avoid — such as materialism, greed, and gossip. This guide, however, is intended not as a lesson plan to be followed exactly, but as a starting point from which parents and teachers can help children explore the ideas in the stories.

The stories have been adapted from the folktales of many peoples. Folktales have long been used throughout the world to guide behaviour by clothing a message or moral in an entertaining story. Some of the well-known Aesop's fables can be traced back to the Jataka tales, a collection of 547 stories

George Ronald, Publisher, 46 High Street, Kidlington, Oxford OX5 2DN, England
 Printed in England ISBN 0-85398-157-4

illustrating passages of Buddhist scripture. And among the Jataka stories are some that are rooted in Indian folktales even older than Buddhism. In later times, the fables spread to Europe, Africa and the Americas, where they became adopted into the folk-tale tradition of their new land, their place of origin forgotten.

'Abdu'l-Bahá often told entertaining stories to illustrate a point. In *Portals to Freedom*, Howard Colby Ives recounts how in 1912, at an international peace conference, 'Abdu'l-Bahá told a party of young people the well-known tale about the mice who decide to tie a bell around the neck of the cat who torments them but cannot agree who should be the one to bell the cat. At the conclusion, Ives says, 'Everyone laughed, 'Abdu'l-Bahá with them. After a short pause he added that that is much like these Peace Conferences. Many words, but no one is likely to approach the question of who will bell the Czar of Russia, the Emperor of Germany, the President of France, and the Emperor of Japan' (p. 196).

Guiding Development

The child's development — physical, intellectual, emotional and spiritual — occurs gradually. For the child, awareness begins with the self and gradually comes to include more and more of the world around the child. At the earliest stage, the individual's view of the world is centred around the self because, at that point in development, the self is all the child knows. As the child gains experience, this simple view of the world becomes modified to take the new experience into account.

Because development occurs in stages, children need to be introduced to ideas and concepts step by step, starting with simple ones and building up to more complex ones. Because no two children are alike, they need to have their educational experiences selected for them according to their own individual needs, and they need to be allowed to learn at their own pace. And, of course, they need adult models to imitate.

Most children learn more when they participate actively rather than passively in the educational process, that is, through talking about things and doing things rather than just listening to an adult telling them what the adult wants them to know. Children need to feel free to ask questions, and the questions they ask often reveal more about their thought processes than the answers they give to questions asked of them. They need to be able to talk over ideas and concepts so that they can come to an understanding of them.

In a talk given in 1913 in Stuttgart, Germany, 'Abdu'l-Bahá said, 'If a plant is carefully nurtured by a gardener, it will become good, and produce better fruit. These children must be given a good training from their earliest childhood. They must be given a systematic training which will further their development from day to day, in order that they may receive greater insight, so that their spiritual receptivity be broadened. Beginning in childhood they must receive instruction. They cannot be taught through books. Many elementary sciences must be made clear to them in the nursery; they must learn them in play, in amusement. Most ideas must be taught them through speech, not by book learning. One child must question the other concerning these things, and the other child must give the answer. In this way, they will make great progress . . . Even so in Godlike affairs. Oral questions must be asked and the answers given orally. They must discuss with each other in this manner.' (*The Bahá'í World*, Vol. IX, p. 543; quoted in *Bahá'í Education*, p. 73)

Using This Guide

Each section of this guide contains questions that can be used to encourage discussion, suggestions for activities, and quotations from the Bahá'í Writings. The questions should not be used to see if the child can produce a 'correct' answer, but rather to encourage discussion — between parent and child, or, if used in a class, among the children themselves. In order to avoid awkwardness or an atmosphere of formality that can inhibit the children's response, adults may find it best to present questions in their own words.

Adults should listen carefully to what each child has to say and should avoid giving children the impression that there is only one possible answer which will be acceptable. Even when children give responses the adult agrees with, they should be encouraged to explain why they gave those particular answers. More important than the content of any answer is the reasoning that led to it and the basic assumptions that underlie it. Children at different developmental levels may give similar answers but for very different, and sometimes opposite, reasons. By explaining the reasoning that has led them to think as they do, parents and children together can examine the foundations of their thinking.

Rather than telling children that their immature

opinions are *wrong* (for they may be quite logical to the child), adults can gently encourage the children to re-examine their opinions by suggesting other ways of looking at the matter in question and pointing out other aspects to consider. As children engage in challenging discussion and are exposed to different points of view, they come to realize that the simple frameworks they have devised to explain the world are inadequate and must be reworked to accommodate the new information.

Children cannot be rushed into learning things that they are not ready for. They must develop at their own pace, but they must also be provided with opportunities for learning so that they *can* develop. While very young children cannot understand a point of view other than their own, for example, unless they are introduced to other points of view they will never be challenged to progress beyond the lower stage. Through exchanging ideas and examining the assumptions underlying their patterns of thinking, children are encouraged to refine their thought processes and move to higher levels of development and understanding.

Parents and teachers should read the stories in advance so they will be able to discuss them in detail with the children. Discussions should be allowed to occur as naturally and comfortably as possible, so that children will feel free to express their thoughts. It is not necessary to use all the questions or do all the activities suggested for each story. Because each child is different — with a different background, different experiences, and at a different level of development — adults should keep in mind the needs and interests of the children, choosing from among the suggested questions and activities or creating new ones as the situation requires. Some of the most fruitful discussion will be that conducted by the children entirely among themselves, and some of the most successful activities will be those the children invent, plan, and carry out.

Creative activities provide an important kind of educational experience — using the imagination and learning by doing. According to their level and their interests, children can 'learn by doing' in any number of ways. Drawing or painting illustrations, dramatizing and miming, planning and putting on puppet shows, making objects and collections, and writing songs and poems are just a few examples. Suggestions for activities are given for each story, but there are endless possibilities for creative activities. Those suggested for one story can often be adapted for other stories.

Frequently the activities suggested make use of the central theme of the story. But many other ideas are introduced in the tales — ideas about the world of nature and other peoples and cultures. Activities do not have to be limited to the main theme. Any aspect that excites children's curiosity to learn can prove a worthwhile path to explore.

Each section of the guide contains quotations from the Bahá'í Writings that touch on themes in the story. While young children may find it difficult to understand the rich and elevated language, they can be exposed to these words of Divine guidance according to their own individual level of understanding. The quotations can be discussed more fully with older children, who can explore the meaning of the words and the significance of the ideas in their own lives.

> Strive thou with heart and soul; see to it that the children are raised up to embody the highest perfections of humankind, to such a degree that every one of them will be trained in the use of the mind, in acquiring knowledge, in humility and lowliness, in dignity, in ardour and love. ('Abdu'l-Bahá, in *Bahá'í Education*, p. 32)

> Children are even as a branch that is fresh and green; they will grow up in whatever way you train them. Take the utmost care to give them high ideals and goals, so that once they come of age, they will cast their beams like brilliant candles on the world . . . (ibid. p. 43)

NEIGHBOURS

Denmark

In this story, a family is friendly to the hill-folk who live nearby, even though the villagers are prejudiced against them and fear them without reason.

Questions to Encourage Discussion

1. How was the family different from the villagers?
2. Why do you think the villagers did not like the hill-people? What would you have done if you were one of the villagers?
3. Did you ever think you wouldn't like a certain kind of food but when you tried it you found it tasted good after all? How many other examples can you give of things you didn't think you would like but found out you liked after all? (For example, a book, a game, a new friend)

Suggestions for Activities

1. Using a library book or an encyclopaedia with coloured pictures of gemstones, can you match the colours of stones mentioned in the story with real precious gems and discover which stones they might be?
2. How many different kinds of people are there in the world? Make a display with pictures cut from magazines to illustrate this statement: 'Ye are the fruits of one tree, and the leaves of one branch.' (Bahá'u'lláh, *Gleanings from the Writings of Bahá'u'lláh*, p. 288)
3. Prejudices are ideas and opinions we form before we really know about something. We all have prejudices — they can be about all kinds of things, including foods, places, occupations, books, individuals or groups of people.

This project can be done individually or by a group working together. Choose a subject you don't know very much about. Before you start your project, write down everything you can think of about this subject. Then put this paper away and don't look at it until you finish your project. Now read about the subject, talk to people who know about it, and find a way — perhaps through a field trip — to experience the subject personally. Afterwards, write down what you know and what you think about the subject now. Take out the paper you wrote before and compare it with what you wrote after you learned about the subject. How have your ideas about the subject changed?

4. Create a poster that will help teach people not to be prejudiced.

Quotations from the Bahá'í Writings

'Prejudices of all kinds, — whether religious, racial, patriotic or political — are destructive of divine foundations in man. All the warfare and bloodshed in human history have been the outcome of prejudice . . . All are the children and servants of God. Why should we be separated by artificial and imaginary boundaries? In the animal kingdom the doves flock together in harmony and agreement. They have no prejudices. We are human and superior in intelligence. Is it befitting that lower creatures should manifest virtues which lack expression in man?' ('Abdu'l-Bahá, *The Promulgation of Universal Peace*, pp. 287–8)

'. . . the entire world of humanity is one tree. The various nations and peoples are the branches of that tree. Individual members of mankind are represented by the twigs and blossoms. Why should these parts of the same tree manifest strife and discord toward each other?' (ibid. p. 373)

THE FOX'S TALE

Scotland

In this story, a fox tricks a gossip-loving duck into becoming the fox's breakfast.

Questions to Encourage Discussion

1. How could the duck have avoided becoming the fox's breakfast?
2. The duck's love of gossip turns out to be deadly to him in the end. How is gossip harmful to people? To the person who is gossiped about? To the person who does the gossiping?
3. Sometimes we call talking about people 'backbiting'. Think about this word. Why do you think it came to be used?
4. What would you do if someone began to say bad things about someone you liked? About someone you didn't like?

Suggestions for Activities

1. Present the story as a puppet show. Make hand puppets for the duck and fox. Don't read or memorize the lines but tell the story in your own words.
2. Make up another animal character the fox might want to have for lunch. But don't let this character listen to the fox's gossip.

3. In real life, many animals trick other animals so they can catch them and eat them. It is part of nature's 'food chain'. Find some examples; what are different ways animals trick other animals into becoming a meal?

Quotations from the Bahá'í Writings

'That seeker should also regard backbiting as grievous error . . . inasmuch as backbiting quencheth the light of the heart, and extinguisheth the life of the soul.' (Bahá'u'lláh, *The Kitáb-i-Íqán*, p. 193)

'. . . magnify not the faults of others that thine own faults may not appear great . . .' (Bahá'u'lláh, *The Hidden Words*, Persian no. 44)

VANYA AND THE RABBIT

Russia

In this story a man sees a rabbit in a ditch and daydreams about how it will give him wealth. But he becomes so absorbed in his dreams that he scares the animal away.

Questions to Encourage Discussion

1. What would Vanya have to have done in order for the story to have a different ending?
2. When do you think daydreaming is good? When do you think it is bad?
3. What do you think about Vanya's scolding his 'sons' for being lazy?
4. It is easy to daydream. Like Vanya, many people just think or talk about what they want to do. Why do you think they just talk about things instead of doing them?

Suggestions for Activities

1. Draw or paint a picture illustrating the story, including what is going on in Vanya's imagination.
2. Think about something you would like to do or make. After you have dreamed about it for a while, make a plan for reaching your goal. Make a list of all the things you will need, and write down all the steps you will need to take, in the order in which you will have to do them. Then begin to carry out your plan.

Quotations from the Bahá'í Writings

'Let deeds, not words, be your adorning.' (Bahá'u'lláh, *The Hidden Words*, Persian no. 5)

'Some men and women glory in their exalted thoughts, but if these thoughts never reach the plane of action they remain useless: the power of thought is dependent on its manifestation in deeds.' ('Abdu'l-Bahá, *Paris Talks*, p. 18)

'The wrong in the world continues to exist just because people talk only of their ideals, and do not strive to put them into practice. If actions took the place of words, the world's misery would very soon be changed into comfort.' ('Abdu'l-Bahá, *Paris Talks*, p. 16)

TUTOKANULA

Miwok (California)

In this story, the animals try to rescue two boys from a high rock. Although the other, larger animals fail, the lowly inch-worm succeeds through perseverance.

Questions to Encourage Discussion

1. Of the animals in the story, which are the strongest and largest? But the smallest and weakest is the hero. Usually we think that to be biggest and strongest is good, and that to be smallest and weakest is bad. But what abilities did the inch-worm have that none of the other animals had?
2. Besides the ability to go up the rock, what good quality helped the inch-worm succeed?
3. What other things could an inch-worm do better than a grizzly bear? How many examples can you think of when size and strength are no help? When is smallness better?
4. What other kinds of 'strength' are there besides physical strength?

Suggestions for Activities

1. Look at a book about Yosemite National Park. Which place do you think the story might be about? Draw or paint a picture of it.
2. Small creatures like worms can have a great effect on other, larger animals. Find some examples of ways in which tiny creatures can affect the lives of larger animals and people.

Quotations from the Bahá'í Writings

'He, verily, shall increase the reward of them that endure with patience.' (Bahá'u'lláh, *Gleanings from the Writings of Bahá'u'lláh*, p. 129)

'Everything of importance in this world demands the close attention of its seeker. The one in pursuit of anything must undergo difficulties and hardships until the object in view is attained and the great success is obtained.' ('Abdu'l-Bahá, *Tablets of 'Abdu'l-Bahá*, p. 265)

HOW ANANSI BECAME A SPIDER

Dagomba (Togo)

In this story, a hunter is kind to a forest gnome who helps him catch all the fish he needs, but Anansi is rude, disobedient, and unkind and goes home empty-handed.

Questions to Encourage Discussion

1. How does the hunter act toward the gnome? How does Anansi act toward him? Why do you think each acts the way he does?
2. When the gnome tells the hunter to take all the fish he wants, the hunter does so. How many reasons can you think of to explain why the hunter does not take the large animals instead of fish?
3. Anansi doesn't want to bother with fish and takes the animals, the crocodiles and hippopotamuses, but this doesn't work. Why not?
4. The hunter shares his food with the strange little gnome who later gives him fish to feed his family. How many reasons can you think of to explain why people share what they have with others?

Suggestions for Activities

1. Imagine you saw one of these signs:

THIS DOOR MUST BE KEPT CLOSED AT ALL TIMES
THIS DOOR MUST BE KEPT OPEN AT ALL TIMES
DO NOT PUSH THIS BUTTON

Make up a story to explain why the sign says what it does and what would happen if someone did not follow the direction, but did the opposite of what the sign says to do. (The action itself must cause something to happen — it is not enough to say that the one who disobeys will be punished.) See how creative you can be.

2. Are you afraid of spiders? Many people are. Can you find out why? By reading and asking experts, see if you can discover if such fear is justified. Make a list of all the other things you can think of that frighten people. Which of these fears are justified and which are not?

Quotations from the Bahá'í Writings

'Look not upon the creatures of God except with the eye of kindliness and of mercy, for Our loving providence hath pervaded all created things, and Our grace encompassed the earth and the heavens.' (Bahá'u'lláh, *Gleanings*, p. 33)

'And among the teachings of Bahá'u'lláh is voluntary sharing of one's property with others among mankind.' ('Abdu'l-Bahá, *Selections from the Writings of 'Abdu'l-Bahá*, p. 302)

'Care for the stranger as for one of your own . . .' (ibid. p. 34)

THE LUCKIEST WOMAN IN THE WORLD

England

In this story, an old woman finds a treasure unexpectedly. Even when she eventually loses it, she is happy and finds something to be thankful for.

Questions to Encourage Discussion

1. How does the old woman feel when the gold turns to silver, then iron, then stone?
2. Most people would say that in the end she lost everything. When we lose something we feel sad. Why isn't the old woman sad? Did she really lose everything? What other kinds of treasure are there besides money?
3. Tell about an experience of yours when something bad happened but it didn't make you sad.

Suggestions for Activities

1. When something is broken or worn out, we usually throw it away. Find something that is cast aside and make something new out of it. (For example, scraps of cloth, paper or yarn; empty containers or boxes; old greetings cards or magazines.) How could you use the object you will create to make someone happy?
2. What if a different person had found the pot in the road — a person who was grumpy and sad instead of cheerful and thankful? Pretend you are that person, and act out the story. How would the story be different?
3. What do you suppose the magical creature that appears at the end of the story looked like? Draw or paint a picture of it.

Quotations from the Bahá'í Writings

'Be generous in prosperity and thankful in adversity.' (Bahá'u'lláh, *Gleanings from the Writings of Bahá'u'lláh*, p. 285)

'The source of all glory is acceptance of whatsoever the Lord hath bestowed, and contentment with that which God hath ordained.' (Bahá'u'lláh, *Tablets of Bahá'u'lláh*, p. 153)

'Anybody can be happy in the state of comfort,

ease, health, success, pleasure and joy; but if one will be happy and contented in the time of trouble, hardship, and prevailing disease, it is the proof of nobility.' ('Abdu'l-Bahá, *Bahá'í World Faith*, p. 363)

THE QUARRELLING QUAIL

India

In this story, a group of quail is threatened by the fowler who tricks them into gathering together so he can net them. Although at first they follow the advice of their leader and work together to outwit the man, once they start to quarrel, their disunity allows the fowler to trap them all.

Questions to Encourage Discussion

1. We know that unity is important to have, but why? Perhaps it will be easier to see why if you think about what happens when you have the opposite of unity — disunity. Describe what would happen if there were disunity in (a) an orchestra, (b) a soccer team, (c) a marching band, (d) a troupe of acrobats, (e) an aeroplane crew.
2. Tell about a time you were in a team — did everyone work together or did some people not do their share? What was the result?
3. What happened when the birds quarrelled? What could they have done differently to avoid quarrelling? After thinking about this, what do you think is necessary in order for a group to stay unified?

Suggestions for Activities

1. Find as many examples as you can of animals that help other animals (their own kind as well as other species) in time of danger.
2. What do you suppose was the special call the leader used to gather the quail together? Make up a rhyme (and set it to a tune you compose yourself) for the leader to use to summon the quail.
3. Present the story as a puppet show (in your own words).

Quotations from the Bahá'í Writings

'This day is the day of union, the day of the ingathering of all mankind. "Verily God loveth those who, as though they were a solid wall, do battle for His Cause in serried lines!"' ('Abdu'l-Bahá, in *Selections from the Writings of 'Abdu'l-Bahá*, p. 260, quoting Qur'án 61:4)

'Every flock of the sheep of God which is protected under the shadow of the Divine Shepherd will not be scattered, but when the sheep are dispersed from the flock, they will necessarily be caught and torn by the wolf.

'Therefore, it is incumbent upon you to flock together! It is incumbent upon you to be united!' ('Abdu'l-Bahá, in *Bahá'í World Faith*, p. 402)

'If love and agreement are manifest in a single family, that family will advance, become illumined and spiritual; but if enmity and hatred exist within it destruction and dispersion are inevitable. This is likewise true of a city. If those who dwell within it manifest a spirit of accord and fellowship it will progress steadily and human conditions become brighter whereas through enmity and strife it will be degraded and its inhabitants scattered. In the same way the people of a nation develop and advance toward civilization and enlightenment through love and accord, and are disintegrated by war and strife. Finally, this is true of humanity itself in the aggregate. When love is realized and the ideal spiritual bonds unite the hearts of men, the whole human race will be uplifted, the world will continually grow more spiritual and radiant and the happiness and tranquillity of mankind be immeasurably increased.' (ibid. pp. 229–30)

COYOTE AND WOODPECKER

Pueblo (New Mexico)

In this story, Coyote imitates the woodpeckers' bright colours but ends up burnt and foolish.

Questions to Encourage Discussion

1. How many reasons can you think of why Coyote might want to pretend to be like the woodpeckers?
2. Do you think the woodpeckers were really trying to show off their feathers? If not, why did Coyote think they were?
3. What are some ways people try to pretend to be something they aren't? Do you think they really believe they are better than other people? Do you think Coyote really believed he was as beautiful as the woodpeckers?

Suggestions for Activities

1. Each animal has some unique quality and is part of Nature's plan — even the coyote. Can you find out some good quality that coyotes have or what part they play in their environment?

2. Make up your own story about a different kind of animal that tries to imitate another animal, or about a person who tries to show that he or she is better than someone else in some way.

Quotations from the Bahá'í Writings

'O Son of Man! Transgress not thy limits, nor claim that which beseemeth thee not.' (Bahá'u'lláh, *The Hidden Words*, Arabic no. 24)

'O Children of Desire! Put away the garment of vainglory, and divest yourselves of the attire of haughtiness.' (ibid. Persian no. 47)

' . . . wish not the abasement of anyone, that thine own abasement be not exposed.' (ibid. Persian no. 44)

THE WONDROUS PILLOW

China

In this story, a man is unhappy with his life until, through the power of a magic pillow, he experiences great wealth and finds that it does not bring contentment.

Questions to Encourage Discussion

1. Chen thinks he will be happy if he is rich, but he finds that wealth does not bring contentment. What problems does Chen have that wealth cannot solve?
2. Suppose you were Chen and suddenly became wealthy. What would you do differently?
3. What do you think Chen meant when he said, 'The greatest treasure of all is contentment'?
4. What sorts of things do you feel people should be content with? What sorts of things should they *not* be content with?

Suggestions for Activities

1. You can make a 'pillow of contentment' for yourself. It doesn't even have to look like a real pillow, as long as you can put things in it. Fill it with sayings and quotations you collect that remind you how to be happy and make you feel better when you're sad. Afterwards, whenever you feel unhappy, you can just look inside your 'pillow'.
2. All over the world, gold and silver are thought of as precious. See if you can find out why this is so. What other kinds of objects have been considered to have special value, in your own culture and in other cultures? What makes such objects 'precious' and 'valuable'? Is it the thing itself that is really special, or do people give those things their 'value'?
3. Look at some library books about Chinese art (or, if possible, visit a museum with a collection of Chinese art). How many objects and characters can you find like those in the story — objects such as porcelain, lacquered furniture, carved jade; characters like the wise old man, peasants, the Emperor, soldiers. See if you can find a picture of an oriental 'pillow' — but don't look for something soft and filled with feathers!

Quotations from the Bahá'í Writings

'O Quintessence of Passion! Put away all covetousness and seek contentment; for the covetous hath ever been deprived, and the contented hath ever been loved and praised.' (Bahá'u'lláh, *The Hidden Words*, Persian no. 50)

'O Ye that Pride Yourselves on Mortal Riches! Know ye in truth that wealth is a mighty barrier between the seeker and his desire, the lover and his beloved. The rich, but for a few, shall in no wise attain the court of His presence nor enter the city of content and resignation . . .' (ibid. Persian no. 53)

'O Son of My Handmaid! Be not troubled in poverty nor confident in riches, for poverty is followed by riches, and riches are followed by poverty. Yet to be poor in all save God is a wondrous gift, belittle not the value thereof, for in the end it will make thee rich in God . . .' (ibid. Persian no. 51)

CLEVER JACKAL

Khoi-Khoi (South Africa)

In this story, a clever jackal gets caught in a trap but talks a monkey into changing places with him.

Questions to Encourage Discussion

1. How did Jackal talk Monkey into taking his place in the trap? What might happen to an animal in a trap? If Monkey knew this, why did he agree to change places with Jackal?
2. Tell what you think might happen after the story ends and Jackal leaves Monkey swinging in the air.
3. What are some ways in which one person might try to get another person to do something they both know they shouldn't do?
4. What are some reasons people agree to do things they know are wrong or harmful?

Suggestions for Activities

1. Make up a story to act out about someone who tries to persuade someone else to do something

harmful. Let the first person try every way he can to talk the second person into it, but don't let the second person give in.
2. Create a poster that will help others to learn not to let people talk them into doing something they shouldn't.

Quotations from the Bahá'í Writings

'Approach not the things which your minds condemn.' (Bahá'u'lláh, *Gleanings from the Writings of Bahá'u'lláh*, pp. 277–8)

'Consider the pettiness of men's minds. They ask for that which injureth them, and cast away the thing that profiteth them. They are, indeed, of those that are far astray . . . That which beseemeth man is submission unto such restraints as will protect him from his own ignorance, and guard him against the harm of the mischief-maker.' (ibid. pp. 335–6)

THE FLIGHT OF THE ANIMALS

Tibet

In this story, a family of hares is frightened by a loud noise and soon has all the other animals in a stampede.

Questions to Encourage Discussion

1. Sudden loud noises can be very startling and frightening. Tell about a time you were scared by a loud noise. What did you think it was? What did it turn out to be?
2. What do you think the hares thought Plop was? What do you think the other, larger animals like the bears and the tigers thought Plop was?
3. Talk about the meaning of these words: rumour, gossip, lie, hearsay. In what ways are they different? In what ways are they similar?
4. In what ways can rumours and gossip do harm (rumours about people; rumours about things)?

Suggestions for Activities

1. Paint or draw a mural of the story starting with the hares in the forest beside the lake (try using shelf lining or wrapping-paper).
2. This game is called 'Telephone'. Those who are playing the game sit in a circle (the more people the better). The first person thinks of a sentence to say and whispers it to the next person, who passes it on to the next person the same way, and so on, until the message has gone around the circle. The last person speaks the message out loud. You may be surprised to hear how the message has changed! After you have played this game for a while, talk about how it shows one of the ways rumours can be harmful, even if they start out as truth.

Quotations from the Bahá'í Writings

'. . . Each must see with his own eyes, hear with his own ears and investigate the truth himself in order that he may follow the truth instead of blind acquiescence and imitation of ancestral beliefs.' ('Abdu'l-Bahá, *The Promulgation of Universal Peace*, p. 454)

SMELLS AND JINGLES

Japan

In this story, a woman enjoys sniffing the aroma of broiled eels, but when the eel-seller tries to charge her for this, she pays with the sound of jingling coins.

Questions to Encourage Discussion

1. Explain why you think it was fair or unfair for the eel-seller to charge the woman for smelling the food. Explain why you think it was just or unjust for the old woman to pay for 'smells' with 'jingles'.
2. If you were the eel-seller, what would you have done?
3. When someone demands something of one unfairly, what can one do?

Suggestions for Activities

1. If you have never eaten eels before, you may not think that they are good to eat. Different cultures have different food preferences. A certain food that one group of people think of as a special treat may not even be considered fit to eat by another group. Find out about the food likes and dislikes of another culture. Compare them with your own. Are there any foods you like which other groups of people do not eat? Can you learn anything about why certain foods are considered special, while others are forbidden?
2. Let one person take the role of the eel-seller, and another person play the other character, who cannot afford to pay for the eels. Let the rest of the group listen to each one explain his or her side of the story, then, among themselves, try to come to a judgement fair to both.

Quotations from the Bahá'í Writings

'Be fair to yourselves and to others, that the

evidences of justice may be revealed, through your deeds, among Our faithful servants. Beware lest ye encroach upon the substance of your neighbour.' (Bahá'u'lláh, *Gleanings from the Writings of Bahá'u'lláh*, p. 278)

'Lay not on any soul a load which ye would not wish to be laid on you, and desire not for any one the things ye would not desire for yourselves.' (ibid. p. 128)

THE MOUSE AND THE MOUNTAIN

Eskimo

In this story a proud little mouse tries to prove how great he is but only makes a fool of himself until he realizes his mistake.

Questions to Encourage Discussion

1. Why do you suppose the mouse thought everything he saw was so large?
2. Compare what the mouse was trying to do at first by swimming the 'lake', cutting the 'tree', and so on, with what he did at the end by carrying the sand to move the mountain.
3. Even the mouse might have found these objects smaller than himself, but for each one can you think of a creature that would find it very large: (a) a teacup, (b) a pebble, (c) a leaf, (d) a drop of water.
4. How do you feel about people who try to show they are better than other people? Have you ever tried to show off, but felt silly afterwards?

Suggestions for Activities

1. Illustrate the story from the tiny mouse's point of view — the blade of grass will look very tall! Now put yourself into the picture. The mouse and the grass will not be so tall any more. See how far your imagination takes you thinking about 'big' and 'small'.
2. The Pyramids, in Egypt, are called one of the wonders of the ancient world. They took many years to build. What other examples can you find of people working long and hard to build monuments or buildings? Compare the reasons behind these building projects, including the Pyramids.

Quotations from the Bahá'í Writings

'Pride not yourselves in your glory, and be not ashamed of abasement. By My beauty! I have created all things from dust, and to dust will I return them again.' (Bahá'u'lláh, *The Hidden Words*, Persian no. 48)

'Humility exalteth man to the heaven of glory and power, whilst pride abaseth him to the depths of wretchedness and degradation.' (Bahá'u'lláh, *Epistle to the Son of the Wolf*, p. 30)

'A man who does great good, and talks not of it, is on the way to perfection.

'The man who has accomplished a small good and magnifies it in his speech is worth very little.' ('Abdu'l-Bahá, *Paris Talks*, p. 16)

THE GOOSE AND THE MOON

Iran

In this story, a goose mistakes moonlight on the surface of the pond for a fish. When a fish finally does appear, she refuses to investigate.

Questions to Encourage Discussion

1. Why does the goose think the moonlight is a fish? How are the two alike and how are they different?
2. Can you think of another way the goose might have tried to find out if it really was a fish? Tell how the story would be different if a different goose came along on a moonlit night looking for fish in the pond.
3. Tell about an experience of yours when you saw something, but it turned out to be something else.
4. Can you think of some ways people might act like the goose and refuse to do something because they have made up their minds about it beforehand?

Suggestions for Activities

1. Using the dictionary and other reference books, list as many words as you can that have to do with seeing something that isn't what it seems. Talk about the words you found. What does each one mean?
2. Can you think of a way this story could be presented as a puppet show? How could you represent the reflection of the moon without using water?

Quotations from the Bahá'í Writings

'The steed of this Valley [the Valley of Search] is patience; without patience the wayfarer on this journey will reach nowhere and attain no goal.' (Bahá'u'lláh, *The Seven Valleys and the Four Valleys*, p. 5)

'Behold, how the divers peoples and kindreds of the earth have been waiting for the coming of the Promised One. No sooner had He, Who is the Sun of Truth, been made manifest, than, lo, all turned away from Him, except them whom God was pleased to guide.' (Bahá'u'lláh, *Gleanings from the Writings of Bahá'u'lláh*, p. 9)

'Man must cut himself free from all prejudice and from the result of his own imagination, so that he may be able to search for truth unhindered.' ('Abdu'l-Bahá, *Paris Talks*, p. 129)

THE TORTOISE THAT TALKED TOO MUCH

India

In this story a tortoise makes friends with two ducks who offer to take him to their home if he can hold on to a stick with his teeth and not speak, but the tortoise cannot remain silent and falls.

Questions to Encourage Discussion

1. The tortoise remembers he mustn't say a word until the last. Something becomes more important to the tortoise than remembering he is supposed to be quiet. What is it?
2. Tell about a time when you wanted to say something but knew you shouldn't — how did you feel about it?
3. How many examples can you give of times when we should not speak, and of times when we should not be silent?

Suggestions for Activities

1. With drawings or paintings, illustrate the story from the tortoise's point of view, in the air.
2. Can you think of any other way the ducks could have carried the tortoise to their home? Illustrate your ideas for air tortoise-transport.
3. A quiet pond or tidepool can be a very interesting place, with more activity than you think. Sit and watch very quietly. Make notes about all the animals you see and what they do. If you can, collect samples of grasses, sand, algae, etc. Draw pictures of the animals you see. (If someone you know has a microscope you can borrow, take a sample of pond water and look at it under the high magnification of the microscope — you'll find there is a lot going on in that tiny drop!) Then make a book about your experiences — everything you saw, heard, smelled, touched, and collected.

Quotations from the Bahá'í Writings

'Blessed are the steadfastly enduring, they that are patient under ills and hardships . . .' (Bahá'u'lláh, *Gleanings from the Writings of Bahá'u'lláh*, p. 129)

'. . . the tongue is a smouldering fire, and excess of speech a deadly poison.' (Bahá'u'lláh, *The Kitáb-i-Íqán*, p. 193)

MANY EARS OF CORN

Maya (Mexico)

In this story, a little girl tries to avoid doing her work, but ends up causing everyone to have to work even harder.

Questions to Encourage Discussion

1. Think about the kinds of work or chores you do in your home. What kinds of work do you like best? What kinds do you like least? Talk about what makes work fun or pleasant, and what makes it unpleasant.
2. Why do people have to work? Some people, like the Mayan girl, say they don't like to work. Why do you think they feel this way? What would you tell them in order to help them?
3. Sometimes when we must do something — or mustn't do something — the reason is not clear until later. Can you think of some examples? Explain how this story is an example.

Suggestions for Activities

1. Often, something one person does affects many people. Make up a story describing all the people who might be affected by the following:
   (a) a nearsighted aeroplane pilot forgets to wear glasses to work
   (b) a bus driver decides to take the day off and goes fishing but doesn't tell anyone
   (c) a cook in a restaurant has a bad cold but comes to work anyway
   (d) the only doctor in a small hospital neglects to check the car tyres, and one day as the doctor is hurrying to work, one tyre goes flat
   (e) a scientist testing a new medicine stays up too late at night and the next morning is too tired to pay close attention to the experiments

See how far your imagination will take you!

2. You can get a feeling for what it is like to make tortillas yourself. Use a recipe for corn or flour tor-

tillas. Try to pat one out by hand first to see what it is like, but you will need to use a tortilla press or a rolling pin to make them very thin and flat. Cook them on an ungreased griddle. Then eat them! How many do you think you would need to make so that everyone in your family could have five at each meal? How long would it take to make them?

Quotations from the Bahá'í Writings

'O My Servants! Ye are the trees of My garden; ye must give forth goodly and wondrous fruits, that ye yourselves and others may profit therefrom. Thus it is incumbent on every one to engage in crafts and professions . . .' (Bahá'u'lláh, *The Hidden Words*, Persian no. 80)

'It is enjoined upon every one of you to engage in some form of occupation, such as crafts, trades and the like. We have graciously exalted your engagement in such work to the rank of worship unto God, the True One.' (Bahá'u'lláh, *Tablets of Bahá'u'lláh*, p. 26)

THE MAGIC TREE

Russia

In this story, a magic tree grants the wishes of a man and his wife; but when they wish to be equal to God, they lose all.

Questions to Encourage Discussion

1. Why couldn't the tree grant their last wish?
2. If you had been the man and had found the magic tree, what would you have done?
3. Why are some people never satisfied with what they have? Is there any time it is good not to be satisfied? What kinds of things shouldn't we be satisfied with?
4. Tell about a time when you wanted something very much, but after you got it, you became tired of it and wanted something else.
5. The man and his wife wanted to be equal to God. Why? Why was it not possible? Is there any way in which people can (and should) try to be 'like' God?

Suggestions for Activities

1. You can see that this story is based on an old tale because there no longer are Czars or nobles in Russia. But the story could take place any time or anywhere. Tell the story in your own words as it could happen in modern times, to modern characters.

Quotations from the Bahá'í Writings

'O Son of Spirit! Ask not of Me that which We desire not for thee, then be content with what We have ordained for thy sake, for this is that which profiteth thee, if therewith thou dost content thyself.' (Bahá'u'lláh, *The Hidden Words*, Arabic no. 18)

'The source of all glory is acceptance of whatsoever the Lord hath bestowed, and contentment with that which God hath ordained.' (Bahá'u'lláh, *Tablets of Bahá'u'lláh*, p. 155)

'. . . man's supreme honour and real happiness lie in self-respect, in high resolves and noble purposes, in integrity and moral quality, in immaculacy of mind. They have, rather, imagined that their greatness consists in the accumulation, by whatever means may offer, of worldly goods.' ('Abdu'l-Bahá, *The Secret of Divine Civilization*, p. 19)

'He hath none to equal Him in the whole universe, nor any partner in all creation.' (Bahá'u'lláh, *Epistle to the Son of the Wolf*, p. 98)

THE MONKEYS' TREASURE

Laos

In this story, a man's generosity and kindness to the monkeys of the forest is rewarded. When his greedy neighbour tries to use trickery to get the reward for himself, he fails.

Questions to Encourage Discussion

1. How is the first man different from other farmers in the way he treats the monkeys? Why do you think he shares his melons with the monkeys?
2. When the man tells his neighbour how he got the gold, the neighbour decides to let the monkeys eat what they wish in his garden too. But what is different about why he does so?
3. Does the neighbour deserve to go to the cave of gold too? Does he deserve to go to the cave of silver? Explain your answer.
4. Tell about an experience you had when you received a reward for doing something good. Explain why you think people should do good deeds, such as being kind to animals. How important is it to receive a reward?

Suggestions for Activities

1. How many wild animals live around you? Think hard! Make a collection of them without capturing them or killing them — but by drawing pictures of them. Put the pictures together to make a book.

2. Choose a kind of animal. Find out all you can about how that animal is helpful to people.
3. Think of something you can do to show kindness to animals. For example, build a bird feeder to feed the wild birds around your home. Using library books about birds, can you identify the birds that come to eat in your fly-in restaurant? Before you decide to do a project like this, think about whether you will want to take responsibility to continue with it, once you begin.

Quotations from the Bahá'í Writings

'Beautify your tongues, O people, with truthfulness, and adorn your souls with the ornament of honesty. Beware, O people, that ye deal not treacherously with anyone.' (Bahá'u'lláh, *Gleanings from the Writings of Bahá'u'lláh*, p. 297)

'. . . withhold not from the poor the gifts which the grace of God hath bestowed upon you. He, verily, shall recompense the charitable, and doubly repay them for what they have bestowed.' (Bahá'u'lláh, *Gleanings from the Writings of Bahá'u'lláh*, p. 278)

'Train your children from their earliest days to be infinitely tender and loving to animals. If an animal be sick, let the children try to heal it, if it be hungry, let them feed it, if thirsty, let them quench its thirst, if weary, let them see that it rests.' ('Abdu'l-Bahá, *Selections from the Writings of 'Abdu'l-Bahá*, p. 159)

THE SUNSHINE TREE

Sweden

In this story a selfish rich man finds that all his wealth cannot get him a poor old woman's marvellous pear tree.

Questions to Encourage Discussion

1. All the rich man's money doesn't get him the Sunshine Tree. How many reasons can you think of to explain this?
2. Why do you think the rich man wanted the old woman's Sunshine Tree when he could grow one of his own from the seed she gave him?
3. Why do you think the Sunshine Tree wanted to live near the old woman in her poor cottage instead of near the rich man and his mansion?
4. How many good things can you think of that cannot be bought with money?

Suggestions for Activities

1. Start a fruit tree from seed. Use seed that comes from a ripe fruit. Some trees, like citrus trees and avocados, can be started in water or in some soil and put in a window for warmth and light. Your tree will need care. When it gets big enough you can transplant it to a bigger pot. Eventually you may even be able to move it outdoors and plant it in your garden. Find out which trees grow best where you live, and what kind of care they require.
2. With some friends, you can make this story into a play. Dramatize it in your own words. Someone can play the part of the Sunshine Tree. You can have fun making props and simple costumes.

Quotations from the Bahá'í Writings

'O Children of Dust! Tell the rich of the midnight sighing of the poor, lest heedlessness lead them into the path of destruction, and deprive them of the Tree of Wealth. To give and to be generous are attributes of Mine; well is it with him that adorneth himself with My virtues.' (Bahá'u'lláh, *The Hidden Words*, Persian no. 49)

'O ye rich ones on earth! If ye encounter one who is poor, treat him not disdainfully. Reflect upon that whereof ye were created.' (Bahá'u'lláh, *Epistle to the Son of the Wolf*, p. 55)

'. . . the happiness and greatness, the rank and station, the pleasure and peace, of an individual have never consisted in his personal wealth, but rather in his excellent character, his high resolve, the breadth of his learning, and his ability to solve difficult problems.' ('Abdu'l-Bahá, *The Secret of Divine Civilization*, pp. 23–4)

Reading List

'Abdu'l-Bahá. *Paris Talks*. London: Bahá'í Publishing Trust, 11th edn 1969.

—— *Promulgation of Universal Peace, The*. Talks Delivered by 'Abdu'l-Bahá during His Visit to the United States and Canada in 1912. Wilmette, Illinois: Bahá'í Publishing Trust, 1982.

—— *Secret of Divine Civilization, The*. Wilmette, Illinois: Bahá'í Publishing Trust, 1957.

—— *Selections from the Writings of 'Abdu'l-Bahá*. Compiled by the Research Department of the Universal House of Justice. Haifa: Bahá'í World Centre, 1978.

—— *Tablets of Abdul-Baha Abbas*. vol. I, New York: Baha'i Publishing Committee, second printing, July 1930. vol. II, Chicago: Baha'i Publishing Society, 1915. vol. III, New York: Baha'i Publishing Committee, second printing 1930.

Bahá'u'lláh. *Epistle to the Son of the Wolf*. Trans. by Shoghi Effendi. Wilmette, Illinois: Bahá'í Publishing Trust, rev. edn 1976.

—— *Gleanings from the Writings of Bahá'u'lláh*. Trans. by Shoghi Effendi. Wilmette, Illinois: Bahá'í Publishing Trust, 2nd rev. edn 1976.

—— *The Hidden Words*. Trans. by Shoghi Effendi. London: Bahá'í Publishing Trust, 1949. Wilmette, Illinois: Bahá'í Publishing Trust, rev. edn 1954.

—— *Kitáb-i-Íqán. The Book of Certitude*. Trans. by Shoghi Effendi. Wilmette, Illinois: Bahá'í Publishing Trust, rev. edn 1974; London: Bahá'í Publishing Trust, 2nd edn 1961.

—— *The Seven Valleys and The Four Valleys*. Trans. by Ali-Kuli Khan (Nabílu'd-Dawlih), assisted by Marzieh Gail. Wilmette, Illinois: Bahá'í Publishing Trust, rev. edn 1952.

—— *The Tablets of Bahá'u'lláh*. Trans. by Habib Taherzadeh with the assistance of a Committee at the Bahá'í World Centre. Haifa: Bahá'í World Centre, 1978.

Bahá'í World Faith. A selection from the Bahá'í Holy Writings. Wilmette, Illinois: Bahá'í Publishing Trust, 1976.

Compilation on Bahá'í Education, Compiled by the Research Department of the Universal House of Justice. Oakham, England: Bahá'í Publishing Trust, 1976.

Ives, Howard Colby, *Portals to Freedom*. Oxford: George Ronald, 1976.